SCHOLASTIC
News
Nonfiction Readers

A Very Busy Firehouse

By Alyse Sweeney

Children's Press®
A Division of Scholastic Inc.
New York Toronto London Auckland Sydney
Mexico City New Delhi Hong Kong
Danbury, Connecticut

These content vocabulary word builders are for grades 1–2.

Reading Consultant: Cecilia Minden-Cupp, PhD, Former Director of the Language and Literacy Program, Harvard Graduate School of Education, Cambridge, Massachusetts

Photographs © 2007: 911 Pictures: 5 top left, 13 (Tom Carter), 5 top right, 9 (Michael Heller), 5 bottom right, 8 (Brian Jenkins); Corbis Images: 17 (First Light), 20 top (Richard Hutchings), 19 (Robert Maass), 23 bottom right (Louis Moses/zefa), 4 bottom right, 10 (Steve Prezant), 20 bottom (Roger Ressmeyer), 23 bottom left (Royalty-Free); Dembinsky Photo Assoc.: 23 top left (Airpack), 2, 5 bottom left, 16 (Michael Messar); Getty Images/Christian Oth: back cover, 4 bottom left, 6; Masterfile/Steve Craft: 1, 4 top, 15; Photo Researchers, NY/Richard Hutchings: 21 top; PhotoEdit/Richard Hutchings: 11; Richard Hutchings Photography: cover, 7; Scott Sroka: 21 bottom; The Image Works/Justin Yrkanin/Syracuse Newspapers: 23 top right.

Book Design: Simonsays Design!
Book Production: The Design Lab

Library of Congress Cataloging-in-Publication Data

Sweeney, Alyse.
   A very busy firehouse / by Alyse Sweeney.
      p. cm. — (Scholastic news nonfiction readers)
   Includes bibliographical references and index.
   ISBN-10: 0-531-16840-9
   ISBN-13: 978-0-531-16840-0
   1. Fire extinction—Juvenile literature. 2. Fire stations—Juvenile literature. I. Title. II. Series.
   TH9148.S94 2007
   628.9'25—dc22   2006015654

1 2 3 4 5 6 7 8 9 10 R 16 15 14 13 12 11 10 09 08 07

CONTENTS

WORD HUNT

Look for these words as you read. They will be in **bold**.

fire axe
(fire ax)

firefighter
(**fire**-fite-ur)

helmet
(**hel**-mit)

fire chief
(fire cheef)

fire truck
(fire truhk)

nozzle
(**noz**-uhl)

siren
(**sye**-ruhn)

Firefighters carefully check all their equipment.

Is each **fire truck** clean? Do the fire trucks have enough gas? Does each **siren** work?

Firefighters make sure they are ready for the next fire.

siren

Weee-ahh
Weee-ahh

Fire trucks need to be cleaned after every fire.

Suddenly, the alarm rings! Firefighters slide down the pole.

They put on their boots, special pants, and coats. Every firefighter also wears a **helmet**. In seconds, the firefighters are on their way!

helmet

Sliding down a pole is faster than taking the stairs.

The **fire chief** decides the best way to fight the fire.

He tells some firefighters to look for people and pets inside the burning building. He tells others to work on putting out the fire.

The fire chief uses a walkie-talkie to tell the firefighters what to do.

Firefighters use a **fire axe** to smash holes in the roof and windows.

The holes let out hot air and smoke. That makes it easier for water to reach the flames.

This fire axe is heavy!

Firefighters must work with a heavy hose.

It takes many firefighters to hold the hose and aim the **nozzle**. The nozzle is where the water blasts out of the hose.

nozzle

Firefighters work together to aim the nozzle straight.

It was a very busy day for the firefighters!

At the end of the day, the firefighters washed the trucks. They washed the hoses. They washed themselves.

Time to rest . . . until the alarm rings again!

YOU'LL SEE MANY THINGS AT A FIREHOUSE!

A **dormitory** is where the firefighters sleep.

A **garage** is where the fire trucks are kept. It is also where the firefighters keep their firefighting clothes.

A **kitchen** is where the firefighters make their food.

A **hose drying tower** is where the hoses are hung to dry. Then they are rolled and put back onto the truck.

YOUR NEW WORDS

fire axe (fire ax) a tool used to fight fires

fire chief (fire cheef) the person who is in charge at a fire

fire truck (fire truhk) a truck that carries equipment for putting out fires

firefighter (**fire**-fite-ur) someone who puts out fires and keeps fires from happening

helmet (**hel**-mit) a hard hat that protects a person's head

nozzle (**noz**-uhl) the end of the hose where the water comes out

siren (**sye**-ruhn) an object that makes a loud sound and is found on fire trucks and ambulances

WHAT ARE OTHER TOOLS A FIREFIGHTER NEEDS?

air pack

face mask

flashlight

rope

INDEX

FIND OUT MORE
Book:
Simon, Seymour. *Fighting Fires*. New York: SeaStar Books, 2002.

Web site:
The Great Sparky the Fire Dog
http://www.sparky.org/

MEET THE AUTHOR:
Alyse Sweeney is a freelance writer who has published more than twenty books and poems for children. Prior to becoming a freelance writer, she was a teacher, reading specialist, and Scholastic editor. Alyse lives in Las Vegas, Nevada, with her husband and two children.